I'M YOUR MAN

Published in 2022 by OH!
An Imprint of Welbeck Non-Fiction Limited,
part of Welbeck Publishing Group.
Based in London and Sydney.
www.welbeckpublishing.com

ISBN 978-1-80069-194-0

Project manager: Russell Porter
Compilation and layout: RH
Editorial: Victoria Godden
Production: Jess Brisley

A CIP catalogue record for this book is available from the British Library

Printed in China

10 9 8 7 6 5 4 3 2 1

Original cover photograph: Yoan Valat/EPA/Shutterstock

THE LITTLE GUIDE TO

LEONARD COHEN

I'M YOUR MAN

CONTENTS

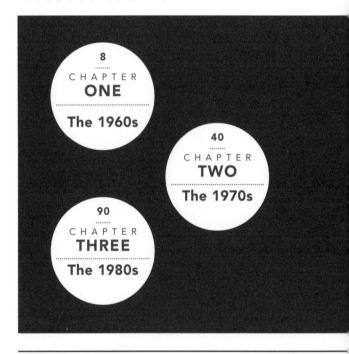

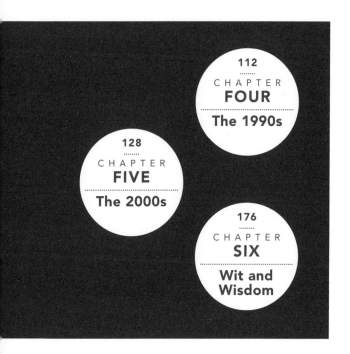

INTRODUCTION

Without a doubt one of the most important, influential and acclaimed artists since the 1960s, Leonard Cohen is admired by fans, musicians and composers the world over. His death in 2016 at the age of 82 was front-page news and he is missed.

The deeply personal nature of his work, and its profound insight into humans and human nature, has seen him hailed as a lyrical genius, and for good reason. His ongoing themes of depression, love, religion and relationships struck a chord with fans all over the world and although his albums (as well as his books of poetry) sold moderately, he achieved true cult status. This book is structured chronologically, making it easy to see how his music, themes and ideas evolved through the years. His look didn't change from the 1980s: the suit, the hat and the guitar.

There are plenty of quotes from the man himself, as well as words from other artists, commentators, critics, collaborators, muses and fans. This book contains many insightful, witty and meaningful quotes by and about Leonard Cohen, as well as a few fascinating facts about him, his life and his music.

Leonard Cohen spent his life searching, experimenting, trying to understand, write down and express the feelings that we all have but are not necessarily able to put into words. He was without doubt one of the great lyricists of his time and is up there with Dylan as one of the popular music icons (although his music almost defies classification – it stands alone). Produced by his son Adam, his last album came out a few years after his death, almost as if he was able to keep his curiosity and questioning going from beyond the grave…

CHAPTER
ONE

THE 1960s

Leonard Cohen
started the decade
as a poet
and ended it as
a musician.

When the chief executive of Columbia Records heard that A&R man John Hammond wanted to sign Cohen in 1967, he reportedly said: 'A 32-year-old poet? Are you crazy?'

Dorian Lynskey
recounts a famous old tale

quoted in Leonard Cohen article by Dorian Lynskey, *The Guardian*, November 11, 2016, theguardian.com

Well, I never thought of myself as a songwriter. I always loved music and I played guitar. I thought of myself as a writer.

Leonard Cohen
on how he views himself

interview with Shelagh Rogers, 2016, brickmag.com

Leonard Cohen's
first book of poems
was published
in 1956, entitled
*Let Us Compare
Mythologies.*

He'd call himself slow. He'd write poems about how Leonard Cohen was a lazy bastard living in a suit.

Leonard Cohen's son **Adam Cohen** on his father's writing process

Scott Timberg interview with Adam Cohen, *The Guardian*, 2018, theguardian.com

During the fifties and sixties
I tried everything I could get my
hands on.

Leonard Cohen
discusses stimulants

interview with Joe Jackson,
Hot Press, 1988, hotpress.com

One of Leonard
Cohen's favourite
poets was
Federico García Lorca;
he even named
his daughter after
the doomed
Spanish writer.

There were no prizes or grants or awards. There weren't even any girls.

Leonard Cohen
on being a recording artist, 1993

theguardian.com

66

On paper, Cohen's music is
astoundingly simple.

99

Brian Howe
alluding to the hidden complexities of
Leonard Cohen's music

Pitchfork, May 4, 2007, pitchfork.com

Songs of Leonard Cohen
(1967)

Side A
Suzanne
Master Song
Winter Lady
The Stranger Song
Sisters of Mercy

Side B
So Long, Marianne
Hey, That's No Way to Say Goodbye
Stories of the Street
Teachers
One of Us Cannot Be Wrong

Songs of Leonard Cohen was more successful in Europe than in the USA, although it eventually achieved gold status in 1989.

John Hammond, the man who signed Leonard Cohen to Colombia Records, was lined up to produce the album, but was ill so John Simon took over.

The back-cover image was bought by Leonard Cohen in a Mexican religious goods shop in New York City.

Not only the cornerstone of Cohen's remarkable career, but also a genuine songwriting landmark in terms of language, thematic developments and even arrangements.

Phil Alexander,
Mojo, on Songs of Leonard Cohen

Mojo, March 2012

66

There are three brilliant songs, one good one, three qualified bummers, and three flaming shits.

99

Arthur Schmidt of *Rolling Stone* with a clinical dissection of *Songs of Leonard Cohen*

review of *Songs of Leonard Cohen* by Arthur Schmidt, *Rolling Stone*, March 9, 1968, rollingstone.com

There's his reedy baritone – a humble, melancholy instrument and an inviting source of warmth.

Brian Howe
Pitchfork review of *Songs of Leonard Cohen*

Pitchfork, May 4, 2007, pitchfork.com

66

Who was this sonorous balladeer, whose songs seemed to be bone-hard fables issuing from some pre-industrial source, and strangely clear-voiced and completely contemporary?

99

Journalist **Andrew Pulver** asks a question that has never really been answered

"My Favourite Album: Songs of Leonard Cohen"
by Andrew Pulver, *The Guardian*, October 6, 2011,
theguardian.com

66

The writing of 'Suzanne,' like all my songs, took a long time. **99**

Leonard Cohen,
to the BBC

quoted in en.wikipedia.org

"

Once created, a great song can exist independently of its creators, taking on a life of its own as it rises to iconic status within the cultural landscape. Such is the case with 'Suzanne.'

"

David Freeland
on the importance of a very famous song

"Behind the Song: Leonard Cohen, 'Suzanne'",
American Songwriter, americansongwriter.com

Flattered somewhat. But I was depicted as I think, in sad terms too in a sense, and that's a little unfortunate.

Suzanne Verdal
on being the subject of the song "Suzanne"

interview with Kate Saunders, *You Probably Think This Song is About You*, BBC Radio 4, June 1998, leonardcohenfiles.com

"

There was a Suzanne who was
associated with the song,
and her name was Suzanne…
She was the wife of a friend of
mine, Armand Vaillancourt.

"

Leonard Cohen
to Shelagh Rogers, 2016

Brick, A Literary Journal, 2016, brickmag.com

I saw him briefly in a hotel and it was a very, very wonderful, happy moment because he was on his way to becoming the great success he is. And the moment arose that we could have a moment together intimately, and I declined.

Suzanne Verdal
on physical intimacy with Leonard Cohen

interview with Kate Saunders, *You Probably Think This Song is About You*, BBC Radio 4, June 1998, leonardcohenfiles.com

❝

'So Long, Marianne' encapsulates Cohen's brilliance, in all its glorious awkwardness.

❞

Journalist **Andrew Pulver**
on the fundamentals of a song

"My Favourite Album: Songs of Leonard Cohen"
by Andrew Pulver, *The Guardian*, October 6, 2011,
theguardian.com

Songs from a Room
(1969)

Side One
Bird on the Wire
Story of Isaac
A Bunch of Lonesome Heroes
The Partisan (Hy Zaret, Anna Marly)
Seems So Long Ago, Nancy

Side Two
The Old Revolution
The Butcher
You Know Who I Am
Lady Midnight
Tonight Will Be Fine

Songs from a Room was produced in Nashville, Tennessee by Simon Johnstone, famous for working with Bob Dylan and Johnny Cash.

"Bird on the Wire" has been covered by Johnny Cash, Joe Cocker, Fairport Convention and Willie Nelson.

The photograph on the back cover is of Marianne Ihlen, and was taken on the Greek island of Hydra.

Songs from a Room is a conceptual departure from *Songs of Leonard Cohen*. It's more eclectic and adventurous.

Dead End Follies
on the Leonard Cohen musical evolution

"Classic Album Review: Leonard Cohen – *Songs From a Room*" by Benoît Lelièvre, January 30, 2020, Dead End Follies, deadendfollies.com

“
It doesn't take a great deal of listening to realize that Cohen can't sing, period. And yet, the record grows on you, and if you give it a chance, it has something to offer.
”

Alec Dubro
of *Rolling Stone* gives Leonard Cohen
some time

"Songs From a Room" by Alec Dubro, *Rolling Stone*,
May 17, 1969, rollingstone.com

Despite his reputation Leonard Cohen's music has always worked best when he's off-kilter, taking wild swings in all directions and letting a scarily plausible red-eyed desperation climb into his music.

Ian Mathers
appreciates Leonard Cohen's work

Songs from a Room review by Ian Mathers, *Stylus Magazine*, May 8, 2007, stylusmagazine.com

"

Cohen's second album, 1969's *Songs from a Room*, was something of a letdown. While it's a fine LP, it ultimately feels neither as striking nor as assured as *Songs of Leonard Cohen*.

Mark Deming
of AllMusic is not a great fan of the second LP

allmusic.com

The song is so important to me.
It's that one verse where I say
that I swear by this song, and by
all that I have done wrong, I'll
make it all up to thee.

Leonard Cohen
on "Bird on the Wire", to *NME*

quoted in "Leonard Cohen – *Songs from a Room*",
On the Record, ontherecord.co

Songs from a Room's strongest moments convey a naked intimacy and fearless emotional honesty that's every bit as powerful as the debut. **99**

Mark Deming,
AllMusic, realizes the LP isn't all bad

allmusic.com

I had some trouble with my first record in getting the kind of music I wanted because I hadn't worked with men for a long time. I had worked by myself and I forgot what was necessary to work with men.

Leonard Cohen
talks about his musical wishes in *Duel*, 1969

quoted in *The Walrus*, November 11, 2016, thewalrus.ca

"

Initially, *Songs from a Room* felt like a trespass. How dare Leonard Cohen dilute the sacred incursion his first album, forged into my being? For some reason, I never considered the possibility of a follow-up.

"

Marina Muhlfriedel

quoted in "Leonard Cohen – *Songs from a Room*", by Harvey Kubernik, as seen on leonardcohenfiles.com

CHAPTER
TWO

THE 1970s

With two cult albums under his belt and a core fanbase in Canada and Europe, Leonard Cohen's literary and musical career developed into the new decade…

"
I am a documentary.

"

Leonard Cohen
offering an explanation of his life and work

interview with Hugh Hebert, *The Guardian*,
August 29, 1970, theguardian.com

"

There's a general conspiracy against lovers, because people really don't like to see other people happy.

"

Leonard Cohen
with an early cynical world view, to
Malka Marom

CBC interview with Malka Marom, 1970,
allanshowalter.com

Songs of Love and Hate
(1971)

Side A
Avalanche
Last Year's Man
Dress Rehearsal Rag
Diamonds in the Mine

Side B
Love Calls You by Your Name
Famous Blue Raincoat
Sing Another Song, Boys
Joan of Arc

Songs of Love and Hate was mostly recorded in Nashville, Tennessee with some additional work in London's Trident Studios.

The album did not reach number one anywhere in the world, but was certified Gold in Canada.

The back cover of the album had no track listing, only a short poem by Leonard Cohen.

The album embraces a brutal honesty that, although daunting on the surface, reminds you that bleakness can be beautiful.

André Dack
review of *Songs of Love and Hate*

"Songs of Love and Hate, Leonard Cohen", audioxide, March 17, 2021, audioxide.com

If there is one thing that Leonard Cohen teaches us, it's that being happy is completely overrated.

Molly Eichel
is ready to learn a lesson

"Leonard Cohen: *Songs of Love and Hate*" by Molly Eichel, Treble, August 29, 2005, treblezine.com

I think [*Songs of Love and Hate*] was gloomy because it was shrouded in loneliness.

John Lissauer,
producer of *Songs of Love and Hate*, on his
first collaboration with Leonard Cohen

"Leonard Cohen's *New Skin for the Old Ceremony* at 45"
by Morgan Enos, Tidal, August 11, 2019, tidal.com

66

Not only is the album conceptually sound, mirroring the same duality that has plagued both Swedenborg and William Blake before him, but the songs, the very breath of oxygen we're seeking, are as astounding as anything he had ever written or would write.

99

Jack Whatley,
Far Out Magazine, is a big fan

"Why *Songs of Love and Hate* is Leonard Cohen's best album" by Jack Whatley, *Far Out Magazine*, March 19, 2021, faroutmagazine.co.uk

Cohen's work actually offers romanticism and wry humour as much as despair.

Tim Nelson
BBC

Tim Nelson review of *Songs of Love and Hate*, 2007, bbc.co.uk

"
There can be no free men unless there are free women.

"

Leonard Cohen
on equality of the sexes

interview with Jack Hafferkamp, *Rolling Stone*,
February 4, 1971, quoted in *Leonard Cohen on Leonard Cohen* edited by Jeff Burger, Omnibus Press, 2014,
books.google.co.uk

Leonard Cohen
recorded an album,
Songs For Rebecca,
with producer
John Lissauer, but it
was never finished
or released.

Be warned though: this is one of the scariest albums of the last forty years with Cohen offering work by turns prophetic ... and suicidal.

Tim Nelson
BBC

Tim Nelson review of *Songs of Love and Hate*, 2007, bbc.co.uk

The hands-down, most heartbreaking moment in an album of heartbreaking moments is 'Famous Blue Raincoat.'

Molly Eichel
sees the misery piling up

"Leonard Cohen: *Songs of Love and Hate*" by Molly Eichel, Treble, August 29, 2005, treblezine.com

"

It was a song I've never been satisfied with. It's not that I've resisted an impressionistic approach to songwriting, but I've never felt that this one, that I really nailed the lyric.

"

Leonard Cohen
is self-critical about "Famous Blue Raincoat"

BBC interview, 1994, quoted in songfacts.com

New Skin for the Old Ceremony (1974)

Side One
Is This What You Wanted?
Chelsea Hotel #2
Lover Lover Lover
Field Commander Cohen
Why Don't You Try

Side Two
There Is a War
A Singer Must Die
I Tried to Leave You
Who By Fire
Take This Longing
Leaving Green Sleeves

"Chelsea Hotel #2" was written about an encounter with Janis Joplin in New York City. Leonard Cohen later apologised to her for revealing it.

The front-cover art for the original album was taken from the ancient book about alchemy, *Rosarium Philosophorum*.

The album never hit the *Billboard* chart in the USA, despite success elsewhere in the world.

I must say I'm pleased with the album. It's good. I'm not ashamed of it and am ready to stand by it. Rather than think of it as a masterpiece, I prefer to look at it as a little gem.

Leonard Cohen sounds happy, to *Melody Maker*'s Harvey Kubernik, 1975

quoted in "August 11: Leonard Cohen – *New Skin for the Old Ceremony*", Born to Listen, August 11, 2018, borntolisten.com

Cohen's fifth album, *New Skin for the Old Ceremony*, is not one of his best, but there are songs on it which will not easily be forgotten.

Paul Nelson,
Rolling Stone, is not taken by the new album

"New Skin for the Old Ceremony" by Paul Nelson, *Rolling Stone*, February 26, 1975, rollingstone.com

"

The crashing crescendo of harpsichord, orchestra and Cohen's screaming makes it an explosive climax to a classic album.

"

Ron Binns is happy with "Leaving Green Sleeves", the Ubyssey, 1975

quoted in "A review of *New Skin for the Old Ceremony*" by Ron Binns, June 11, 2011, leonardcohenforum.com

Leonard Cohen
first played
at the Montreux
Jazz Festival
in 1976.

The lyrics are filled with abstract yet vivid images, and the album primarily uses the metaphor of love and relationships as battlegrounds.

Vik Lyengar, AllMusic, recounting Leonard Cohen's favourite themes

"New Skin for the Old Ceremony Review" by Vik Iyengar, All Music, allmusic.com

"

For a while, I didn't think there was going to be another album. I pretty well felt that I was washed up as a songwriter because it wasn't coming anymore.

"

Leonard Cohen, showing early signs of trouble in the creative process, 1975

"Leonard Cohen: Cohen's New Skin" by Harvey Kubernik, *Melody Maker*, March 1, 1975, rocksbackpages.com

The kind of sensibility I've been influenced [by], of course, [is] a great deal by the French writers – Camus, Sartre – the Irish poets – Yeats – the English poets…

Leonard Cohen on his key influences in poetry an philosophy, 1974

Quoted in "Leonard Cohen speaks in 1974 on the wild and winding paths of the creative process", That Eric Alper, June 16, 2017, thatericalper.com

"

Leonard's songs felt cinematic
to me.

"

John Lissauer,
co-producer of *New Skin for the Old
Ceremony*, talking about the song's suitability
for a movie

Venice Film Festival 2021 review by Stephen Saito,
The Moveable Fest, September 2, 2021, moveablefest.com

66

I thought he'd be this dark, depressed, moody folky guy with his minor key songs. But there was no age difference between us, even though he was probably 18 years older. We were like kids. He was giggly.

99

John Lissauer
shows apprarences can be deceiving

"Leonard Cohen's *New Skin for the Old Ceremony* at 45"
by Morgan Enos, Tidal, August 11, 2019, tidal.com

Songs seem to take me a long time. I don't know why; they're not especially excellent for taking so long. I don't have any sense or urgency about any of my writing actually. I don't think mankind will be damaged if I don't put out a new album or a new book. **99**

Leonard Cohen
on the songwriting process, *Sounds*, 1976

interview with Mick Brown, *The Guardian*, September 17, 2014, theguardian.com

Death of a Ladies' Man
(1977)

Side One
True Love Leaves No Traces
Iodine
Paper Thin Hotel
Memories

Side Two
I Left a Woman Waiting
Don't Go Home with Your Hard-On
Fingerprints
Death of a Ladies' Man

Phil Spector produced the album with Leonard Cohen, and recording took place in three different studios, with a vast number of backing musicians.

To Leonard Cohen's surprise, Phil Spector did the final mixing by himself, as he had done when recording with John Lennon.

The backing vocals on "Don't Go Home with Your Hard-On" are by Bob Dylan and Allen Ginsberg, who were persuaded to sing by Spector.

People were skating around on bullets, guns were finding their way into hamburgers, guns were all over the place. It wasn't safe. It was mayhem, but it was part of the times. It was rather drug-driven.

Leonard Cohen
on recording *Death of a Ladies' Man*

interview with Adrian Deevoy, Q magazine, 1991, en.wikipedia.com

"

Death of a Ladies' Man is a difficult and wholly unique beast of an album. **"**

John Paul,
Spectrum Culture, on the fundamentals

"Revisit: Leonard Cohen: *Death of a Ladies' Man*"
by John Paul, April 27, 2021, spectrumculture.com

Too much of the record sounds like the world's most flamboyant extrovert producing and arranging the world's most fatalist introvert.

Paul Nelson,
Rolling Stone, is not a big fan

"Death of a Ladies' Man" by Paul Nelson, *Rolling Stone*, February 9, 1978, rollingstone.com

66

He had a bottle of wine in one hand and a 35mm pistol in the other. He put his arm around my shoulder, pressed the muzzle into my neck and said, 'Leonard, I love you.' At which point I said: 'I hope you really do, Phil.'

99

Leonard Cohen
on the dangers of recording with Phil Spector

'I never discuss my mistresses or my tailors', interview
with Nick Paton Walsh, *The Observer*, October 14, 2001,
theguardian.com

Death of a Ladies' Man is certainly not for everyone (particularly the faint of heart) and requires a great deal of investment on the part of the listener.

John Paul
discusses Leonard Cohen's most controversial LP

"Revisit: Leonard Cohen: Death of a Ladies' Man" by John Paul, April 27, 2021, spectrumculture.com

"

A cursory listen to the album suggests that the whole thing was simply a ragbag of crazy notions thrown into the air to see where they landed.

"

Dave Thompson, All Music,
is possibly not a big fan of *Death of a Ladies' Man*

allmusic.com

His career then took a decided turn for the worse with the disappointing *Death of a Ladies' Man* (1977), a collaboration with legendary producer Phil Spector, whose grandiose style was ill suited to Cohen's understated songs.

Encyclopaedia Britannica

britannica.com

Leonard Cohen released a volume of poetry in 1978, ***Death of a Lady's Man.***

Recent Songs
(1979)

Side One
The Guests
Humbled in Love
The Window
Came So Far for Beauty
The Lost Canadian (Un Canadien errant)

Side Two
The Traitor
Our Lady of Solitude
The Gypsy's Wife
The Smokey Life
Ballad of the Absent Mare

Recent Songs was regarded as a return to form for Leonard Cohen after the controversial *Death of a Ladies' Man*.

The painting on the cover is by American artist Dianne V. Lawrence. Leonard Cohen said, "I don't have many paintings, but I have three of hers."

Recent Songs was one of Leonard Cohen's personal favourite albums, according to an interview he did with Sylvie Simmons for *Mojo* in 2001.

Sessions started in the afternoon and we'd go into the evenings. No drinking, that I saw, no visitors. Finished at a reasonable time, no early hours stuff.

John Bilezikjian, musician on *Recent Songs* to Anthony Reynolds, author of *Leonard Cohen: A Remarkable Life*

quoted in Wikipedia, en.wikipedia.org

"

Leonard Cohen has finally learned to use music as another kind of paint.

"

Debra Rae Cohen, *Rolling Stone*, on Leonard Cohen's new direction

Recent Songs review by Debra Rae Cohen, *Rolling Stone*, February 21, 1980, rollingstone.com

I think I like *Recent Songs*
the best.

Leonard Cohen
to *Mojo* magazine, 2001

interview with Sylvie Simmons, 2001, quoted in
"This is Leonard Cohen's favourite Leonard Cohen album"
by Joe Taysom, *Far Out Magazine*, October 8, 2020,
faroutmagazine.co.uk

> If not Cohen's most provocative collection, *Recent Songs* is one of his most confident and surefooted, and it came as a relief to fans alienated by his mid-seventies dive into decadence.

Stereogum
on Leonard Cohen's favourite album

"Leonard Cohen Albums From Worst to Best"
by Zach Schonfeld, *Stereogum*, November 15, 2016,
stereogum.com

The accents of the East spice the rhythms of the West, while medieval symbols and modern language combine to let the songs swing free in time as well as space.

Debra Rae Cohen, *Rolling Stone*, is appreciative of the original mixture of influences on *Recent Songs*

Recent Songs review by Debra Rae Cohen, *Rolling Stone*, February 21, 1980, rollingstone.com

My last album was called *Recent Songs* and that was the most perfect title I've ever come up with.

Leonard Cohen
on album titles

Interview with Patricia Keeney and Robert Sward,
CBC Radio, 1984, leonardcohenfiles.com

66

Musically, it marked a return to the gypsy folk sound of his early records after the incongruous arrangements Phil Spector imposed on its predecessor.

99

William Ruhlmann,
All Music, on *Recent Songs*

allmusic.com

"

There's not a cut on *Recent Songs* without something to offer… and at least four or five tunes are full-fledged masterpieces.

"

Debra Rae Cohen,
Rolling Stone, is keen on the album

Recent Songs review by Debra Rae Cohen,
Rolling Stone, February 21, 1980, rollingstone.com

Recent Songs was more than just a record of flawless songs. It confirmed that he was an artist truly like no other and people were wrong for ever writing him off for even a millisecond.

Joe Taysom, *Far Out Magazine*, on the enduring popularity of *Recent Songs*

"This is Leonard Cohen's favourite Leonard Cohen album" by Joe Taysom, *Far Out Magazine*, October 8, 2020, faroutmagazine.co.uk

"

Like Cohen, the hero is a footsore soldier of the sex wars, a true believer who nevertheless wishes he'd already found the damn Grail.

"

Debra Rae Cohen
Rolling Stone, on "The Traitor"

Recent Songs review by Debra Rae Cohen, *Rolling Stone*, February 21, 1980, rollingstone.com

CHAPTER
THREE

THE 1980s

A five-year gap
between albums saw
Leonard Cohen
embrace the new decade
musically with a
popular but challenging
new direction…

I have a cult and we have strange rituals ... the only person I see is Howard Hughes.

Leonard Cohen
[laughing] on his "cult"

interview on *The Don Lane Show*, 1980,
youtube.com

"
The longing exists on a conscious level but the deployment of the energies is somehow illuminated through the work. I know that I want to be in one place. **"**

Leonard Cohen
on not moving around for a while

interview on *Authors* with Patrick Watson, 1980,
cbc.ca

Various Positions
(1984)

Side One
Dance Me to the End of Love
Coming Back to You
The Law
Night Comes On

Side Two
Hallelujah
The Captain
Hunter's Lullaby
Heart with No Companion
If It Be Your Will

Leonard Cohen published no new songs or written work between 1979 and 1984, but he did write and star in a musical, *I Am a Hotel*, for Canadian television.

Various Positions was produced by John Lissauer, who worked on *New Skin for the Old Ceremony*. He and Leonard Cohen created an album, *Songs For Rebecca*, that has never been released.

"Hallelujah" has been a much more successful song for other artists, covered by John Cale, Jeff Buckley and Alexandra Burke, among others.

66

Recorded with vocalist Jennifer Warnes ... *Various Positions* is a stunning return to form.

99

Jason Ankeny,
All Music, appreciates the new album

Various Positions Review by Jason Ankeny,
allmusic.com

In 1984,
Leonard Cohen
wrote a musical called
Night Magic
with Lewis Furey.

Various Positions is less satisfying than *Recent Songs* or *New Skin for the Old Ceremony* (though superior to *Death of a Ladies' Man*). 🙴

Don Shewey,
Rolling Stone, compares albums

Various Positions review by Don Shewey, *Rolling Stone*, June 20, 1985, rollingstone.com

"

Various Positions proved to be a transitional album for Cohen, poised halfway between the classic balladic style of *Recent Songs* and the cool electronic backing of *I'm Your Man.*

"

Rough Trade
review of *Various Positions*

roughtrade.com

Columbia Records mogul Walter Yetnikoff declined even to release 1984's *Various Positions* (the one with 'Hallelujah'), reportedly explaining: 'Look, Leonard, we know you're great, but we don't know if you're any good.'

Dorian Lynskey, *The Guardian*, with a great story

"Leonard Cohen: All I've got to put in a song is my own experience" by Dorian Lynskey, *The Guardian*, January 19, 2012, theguardian.com

"

When Leonard released 'Hallelujah' in 1984 on his album *Various Positions*, the album [had] hardly any fanfare, and nobody seemed to notice.

"

Paul Zollo discusses what became one of Leonard Cohen's most famous songs

"Dylan sings 'Hallelujah' and the Praises of Leonard Cohen" by Paul Zollo, American Songwriter, americansongwriter.com

I'm Your Man
(1988)

Side One
First We Take Manhattan
Ain't No Cure For Love
Everybody Knows
I'm Your Man

Side Two
Take This Waltz
Jazz Police
I Can't Forget
Tower of Song

I'm Your Man was recorded in Los Angeles, USA, Paris, France and Montreal, Canada.

I'm Your Man was the first of Leonard Cohen's albums where he was the sole producer.

The front-cover photograph of Leonard Cohen eating a banana was photographed by publicist Sharon Weisz.

I'm Your Man reinvented Leonard Cohen at age 53. It is the most fun you can have while being told that life is a terrible joke.

Dorian Lynskey, *Pitchfork*, on the first of many Leonard Cohen reinventions

"Leonard Cohen *I'm Your Man*" by Dorian Lynskey, *Pitchfork*, November 20, 2016, pitchfork.com

"

Older and wiser, Cohen began to own the sad-eyed malaise as an affectation instead of chronic condition.

"

Liz Itkowsky, Albumism, reports on the development of Leonard Cohen

"Leonard Cohen's *I'm Your Man* turns 30" by Liz Itkowsky, Albumism, February 2, 2018, albumism.com

I'm Your Man is such an amazingly high quality Leonard Cohen album that fully six of its eight tracks are included on his greatest hits compilation.

Norman Records

normanrecords.com

66

It's not an uplifting album, but it's a strangely reassuring one, because you feel that Cohen is working like a dog on the listener's behalf to make the intolerable tolerable.

99

Dorian Lynskey,
Pitchfork, has conflicted views

"Leonard Cohen *I'm Your Man*" by Dorian Lynskey,
Pitchfork, November 20, 2016, pitchfork.com

A stunningly sophisticated leap into modern musical textures, *I'm Your Man* re-establishes Leonard Cohen's mastery.

Jason Ankeny,
All Music, likes the new direction

I'm Your Man review by Jason Ankeny,
AllMusic, allmusic.com

"

I think it was much easier for a lot of people in America to get into. In Britain and Europe, people love that kind of darker music. **"**

Sylvie Simmons, author of biography *I'm Your Man*, on the album of the same name

"Leonard Cohen's *I'm Your Man* Album Turns 30" by Ron Hart, *Billboard*, February 2, 2018, billboard.com

It's gotten deeper, it's about
a hundred thousand cigarettes
deeper.

Leonard Cohen
on his voice changing, 1988

interview with John Archer on BBC television,
1988, youtube.com.

"

I don't think that anybody has a fixed self, I think that everybody is continually moving into all different kinds of characters or roles ... it doesn't aggravate my normal sense of schizophrenia.

"

Leonard Cohen
on his various personas, 1988

interview on *Kulturen*, Sweden, 1988,
youtube.com.

CHAPTER
FOUR

1990s

Newly established
on bookshelves, turntables
and dancefloors and
with an expanding audience,
Leonard Cohen's output
increased towards
the end of the millennium.

66

Yes I've been blackening pages, here and there, and scratching away.

99

Leonard Cohen
on whether he'll have a new album
out soon, 1997

interview with Chris Doritos, KCRW FM,
February 18, 1987, leonardcohenfiles.com

" I've been working on this lyric for about a year now. I wanted it to have the feel of an old folk song. "

Leonard Cohen
discussing his lengthy songwriting process, 1995

"At lunch with Leonard Cohen" by John Pareles, *The New York Times*, October 11, 1995, nytimes.com

The Future
(1992)

Track list
The Future
Waiting for the Miracle
Be for Real
Closing Time
Anthem
Democracy
Light as the Breeze
Always
Tacoma Trailer

The Future was one of Leonard Cohen's bestselling albums in the USA, where sales had been traditionally low; it went double-platinum in Canada.

Songs from *The Future* were used in the films *Natural Born Killers*, *The Life of David Gale* and *Wonder Boys*.

In 1993 Leonard Cohen won a Juno Award for Best Male Vocalist, for *The Future*.

"

I asked myself is democracy really coming to the East?

"

Leonard Cohen
on the song "Democracy"

Leonard Cohen interview with David Dye, 1993,
allanshowalter.com

"
Whenever anything of that gravity is delivered it's hard to put it on the coffee table...

"

Leonard Cohen
on his bleak outlook

The Future interview, 1993, conducted by Barbara Gowdy,
soundcloud.com

The Future, Cohen's eleventh album, is epic.

Christian Wright,
Rolling Stone, in positive mood

"The Future" by Christian Wright, *Rolling Stone*,
January 7, 1993, rollingstone.com

"

I asked myself, 'Where is democracy really coming?' And it was the U.S.A... This is really where the races confront one another, where the classes, where the genders, where even the sexual orientations confront one another. This is the real laboratory of democracy.

"

Leonard Cohen
on the song "Democracy"

From an interview with Paul Zollo for his book
Songwriters On Songwriting

"

From about '75 to '85 there wasn't much interest at all. In fact, my name was a kinda joke…

"

Leonard Cohen
to Dave Fanning, on dark times

Leonard Cohen interview with Dave Fanning,
1993, fanningsessions.wordpress.com

66

If something works, you do it over and over again… If the thing works, we do it until it stops working.

99

Leonard Cohen
to MTV, on continuing to record and tour

interview with MTV, 1993, YouTube,
youtube.com

As they say in rock n roll, they don't pay you to sing, they pay you to travel.

Leonard Cohen
on life on the road, 1993

Leonard Cohen interview with David Dye, 1993,
allanshowalter.com

"

The Future might as easily have been a book: A more troubling, more vexing image of human failure has not been written.

"

Christian Wright, *Rolling Stone*,
on the bleakness of *The Future*

"The Future" by Christian Wright, *Rolling Stone*,
January 7, 1993, rollingstone.com

I had a clear sense this was going to produce a lot of suffering.

Leonard Cohen
on the fall of the Berlin Wall, 1993

Leonard Cohen interview with David Dye, 1993,
allanshowalter.com

66

The sixties lasted about fifteen minutes.

99

Leonard Cohen
to MTV, on looking back

interview with MTV, 1993, YouTube,
youtube.com

CHAPTER
FIVE

THE 2000s

A steady output
of poetry, prose, music
and performance
marked the two final
decades of
Leonard Cohen's life.

Theology or religious speculation bears the same relationship to real experience as pornography does to lovemaking. They're not entirely unconnected. I mean, you can get turned on.

Leonard Cohen
on certain similarites…

"At lunch with Leonard Cohen" by John Pareles, *The New York Times*, October 11, 1995, nytimes.com

"

No one writes about a lot of things the way Cohen did, including spirituality and death.

"

Eric R. Danton,
Paste magazine, on Leonard Cohen's originality

"Leonard Cohen Remains Indispensable on Thanks for the Dance" by Eric R. Danton, *Paste magazine*, November 19, 2019, pastemagazine.com

Ten New Songs
(2001)

Track list
In My Secret Life
A Thousand Kisses Deep
That Don't Make It Junk
Here It Is
Love Itself
By the Rivers Dark
Alexandra Leaving
You Have Loved Enough
Boogie Street
The Land of Plenty

Ten New Songs was Leonard Cohen's first album in almost ten years. He had been in the Mt. Baldy Zen Center near Los Angeles with his Zen Master Roshi for five of them.

Sharon Robinson co-wrote, produced and co-arranged the entire album.

Ten New Songs was Leonard Cohen's first album to be recorded entirely digitally.

There's a kind of pulse,
an invitation to get into it –
a groove.

Leonard Cohen
on *Ten New Songs*

"I never discuss my mistresses or my tailors", interview
with Nick Paton Walsh, *The Observer*, October 14, 2001,
theguardian.com

Ten New Songs
was recorded at
Still Life Studio –
Leonard Cohen's and
Sharon Robinson's
home studio.

66

Lilting Lenny serves us a diet of sex, love and ageing.

99

Chris Jones,
BBC, 2002

Ten New Songs review, bbc.co.uk

"

A ghostly soundscape populated by the usual cavalcade of beautiful losers. Only now, with age, the bloody literary machine cuts even deeper.

"

Steven Chean, *Rolling Stone*, on the darkening themes behind Leonard Cohen's work

"Ten New Songs" by Steven Chean, *Rolling Stone*, October 9, 2001, rollingstone.com

Yet in the new album, *Ten New Songs*, Cohen seems to have reinvented himself. Gone is the anxiety of the last 50 years, and the one-liners of the past decade.

Nick Paton Walsh
on Leonard Cohen's new direction

"I never discuss my mistresses or my tailors", interview with Nick Paton Walsh, *The Observer*, October 14, 2001, theguardian.com

66

There are moments where
I wonder if he hasn't gone over
the edge into helplessness, letting
his inner conflicts have their way
with him.

99

Pitchfork
review of *Ten New Songs*

review by Dominique Leone, *Pitchfork*,
November 4, 2001, pitchfork.com

Dear Heather
(2004)

Track list
Go No More A-Roving
Because Of
The Letters
Undertow
Morning Glory
On That Day
Villanelle for Our Time
There for You
Dear Heather
Nightingale
To a Teacher
Tennessee Waltz
(Live at Montreuz Jazz Festival)

Three of the songs on
Dear Heather were from the *Ten
New Songs* sessions.

Dear Heather was Cohen's highest-
charting US album since 1969.

There was no tour to support
Dear Heather and Leonard Cohen
did no interviews around the
album either.

If this is indeed his final offering as a songwriter, it is a fine, decent, and moving way to close this chapter of the book of his life.

Dear Heather review by **Thom Jurek**, All Music

allmusic.com

"

There is also a distinct sense of directness and finality about many of the lyrics. Cohen declined to do any interviews because, he claims, the album speaks for itself and there is nothing more to add.

"

Alexis Petridis,
The Guardian, dissects the words

"Leonard Cohen, *Dear Heather*" by Alexis Petridis,
The Guardian, October 22, 2004, theguardian.com

Really, we can only hope that this isn't the end of Leonard's story. There must be more. But if this is the end, then I'm sorry to report that *Dear Heather* is a particularly dour, unsatisfying way to end such an intriguing career. 99

Stylus magazine
2004

stylusmagazine.com

In 2005, Leonard Cohen sued his former manager for misappropriation of $5m of his retirement funds. The loss of revenue forced him back on the road...

The tinny, ersatz backing actually makes Cohen's oak-aged, lugubrious baritone seem more resonant than ever.

The Times
2004

timesonline.co.uk

"

Leonard Cohen has had No Voice since he began recording at 33. But he has more No Voice today, at 70, than he did on *Ten New Songs*, at 67.

"

Robert Christgau, *The Village Voice*, notes the evolution of Leonard Cohen's voice, 2004

robertchristgau.com

Old Ideas
(2012)

Track list
Going Home
Amen
Show Me the Place
Darkness
Anyhow
Crazy to Love You
Come Healing
Banjo
Lullaby
Different Sides

Old Ideas topped the charts in 11 countries, including Finland, where Cohen became (at 77) the country's oldest person to have a number-one album.

Old Ideas was Leonard Cohen's highest chart album in the US, reaching number three.

Old Ideas is one of Leonard Cohen's most critically acclaimed albums.

The vocals and music unfold in a whisper, and each cut waits tremulously for the dawn, with no guarantee that this time the darkness will not be permanent.

Joe Levy, *Rolling Stone*, on the sense of impending doom that pervades *Old Ideas*

"Old Ideas" by Joe Levy, *Rolling Stone*, January 26, 2012, rollingstone.com

"
Old Ideas is a spare, low-key album rooted in blues and gospel – maybe the closest thing he's made to 'folk' music since the early seventies.

"

Mike Powell, *Pitchfork*, on whether Leonard Cohen is going back to his roots

"Leonard Cohen *Old Ideas*" by Mike Powell, *Pitchfork*, February 1, 2012, pitchfork.com

66

Old Ideas is not all about death, betrayal and God, juicy as these are. As the title suggests, it is more of the stuff that has made Cohen indispensable for six decades: desire, regret, suffering, misanthropy, love, hope, and hamming it up.

99

Kitty Empire,
The Observer, traces Leonard Cohen's key themes

"Leonard Cohen: *Old Ideas* – review" by Kitty Empire, *The Observer*, January 22, 2012, theguardian.com

In 2008,
Leonard Cohen
was inducted
into the
**Rock and Roll
Hall of Fame**.

Popular Problems
(2014)

Track list
Slow
Almost Like the Blues
Samson in New Orleans
A Street
Did I Ever Love You
My Oh My
Nevermind
Born in Chains
You Got Me Singing

Popular Problems was a top-ten album in most countries around the world. The USA (number 15) was an exception.

Popular Problems was produced and co-written by Patrick Leonard, best known for his work with Madonna.

"Nevermind" was originally published as a poem, in 2005.

In *Popular Problems*, his thrilling new studio album, Leonard Cohen gets down into the avenues of our dreams and sets a new tone and speed of hope and despair, grief and joy.

Press release, 2014

web.archive.org

"

With his newest album, *Popular Problems* …it seems that the only thing that will stop Cohen's creative surge is the drop of the final curtain. And I'm sure he'll have plenty to report back to us while it's coming down.

"

Douglas Heselgrave, *Paste* magazine, with the realization that Leonard Cohen is here to stay

"Leonard Cohen: *Popular Problems* Review" by Douglas Heselgrave, *Paste* magazine, September 23, 2014, pastemagazine.com

Popular Problems flies by, with only nine songs in 36 minutes. Yet the music creates a space for reflection that expands with each listen.

Ann Powers,
NPR, on the depth of the album

"First listen: Leonard Cohen, *Popular Problems*"
by Ann Powers, September 15, 2014,
npr.org

Leonard Cohen is
mentioned in songs by
Nirvana, Lloyd Cole &
the Commotions and
Marillion.

You Want It Darker
(2016)

Track list
You Want It Darker
Treaty
On the Level
Leaving the Table
If I Didn't Have Your Love
Traveling Light
It Seemed the Better Way
Steer Your Way
String Reprise/Treaty

You Want It Darker was released just 17 days before Leonard Cohen died.

The title track, "You Want It Darker" won a Grammy Award for Best Rock Performance in 2018.

Leonard Cohen's parts were recorded in the living room of his Los Angeles home.

I said I was ready to die recently. And I think I was exaggerating. I've always been into self-dramatization. I intend to live for ever.

Leonard Cohen
to the audience at a listening party for
You Want It Darker

"Leonard Cohen: *You Want It Darker* review"
by Alexis Petridis, *The Guardian*, October 20, 2016,
theguardian.com

"

As I approach the end of my life, I have even less and less interest in examining what have got to be very superficial evaluations or opinions about the significance of one's life or one's work. I was never given to it when I was healthy, and I am less given to it now.

"

Leonard Cohen
as self-aware as ever

"Leonard Cohen makes it darker" by David Remnick,
The New Yorker, October 10, 2016, newyorker.com

This is an album of killer couplets, even the bleakest delivered with a half-smile. Finality is a theme.

Kitty Empire,
The Obverver, thinks this could be Leonard Cohen's last album

"Leonard Cohen: *You Want It Darker* review"
by Kitty Empire, *The Observer*, October 23, 2016,
theguardian.com

You Want It Darker
was a number-one
hit in 14 countries,
including the USA and
Canada.

We're actually not that tight a family, but I have expressed my gratitude to my son many times ... and it was a great privilege to have someone of this skill bringing this album to conclusion.

Leonard Cohen

Press conference for *You Want It Darker*, Los Angeles, October 13, 2016, youtube.com

66
As far as I know, no one else comes close to this in modern music. His gift or genius is in his connection to the music of the spheres.
99

Bob Dylan
on Leonard Cohen

"Dylan sings 'Hallelujah' and the Praises of Leonard Cohen"
by Paul Zollo, American Songwriter,
americansongwriter.com

What is remarkable about 'The Flame,' 'You Want It Darker' and now 'Thanks for the Dance' is the clarity and self-awareness with which Cohen wrestles with his own impending death.

Lindsay Zoladzm, *The New York Times*, thinks Leonard Cohen is approaching the end of his time

"A Last Dance for Leonard Cohen" by Lindsay Zoladz, *The New York Times*, November 19, 2019, nytimes.com

"

During the final years ... Cohen published a book of poetry, toured the whole goddamn world ... headlined Coachella, completed his first new album in seven years, toured the world yet again, and then released two more albums of excellent quality just two years apart.

"

Stereogum
is in awe of Leonard Cohen's late-in-life achievements

"Leonard Cohen Albums From Worst to Best" by Zach Schonfeld, Stereogum, November 15, 2016, stereogum.com

Thanks For the Dance
(2019)

Track list
Happens to the Heart
Moving On
The Night of Santiago
Thanks for the Dance
It's Torn
The Goal
Puppets
The Hills
Listen to the Hummingbird

Thanks For the Dance was released almost exactly three years after Leonard Cohen's death.

The vocal tracks were recorded as part of the *You Want It Darker* sessions.

The album was finished by Leonard Cohen's son, Adam Cohen.

A cult icon in songwriting, that anxious, nagging desire to write is something Cohen spoke of as both a struggle and a blessing – and one which is beautifully poignant in this compilation of songs.

Esme Bennett, *The Quietus*, is deeply appreciative of Leonard Cohen's perseverance

"Sketches In Eternity: Leonard Cohen's *Thanks For The Dance*" by Esme Bennett, *The Quietus*, November 14, 2019, thequietus.com

"

In composing and arranging the music for his words, we chose his most characteristic musical signatures, in this way keeping him with us.

"

Adam Cohen
on continguing the legacy

statement by Adam Cohen, quoted in "Sketches In Eternity: Leonard Cohen's *Thanks For the Dance*" by Esme Bennett, *The Quietus*, November 14, 2019, thequietus.com

This gentle collection justifies its existence with a cathartic energy that offers closure.

Thomas Hobbs,
NME, thinks that's it for Leonard Cohen recordings

review by Thomas Hobbs, *NME*,
November 19, 2019, nme.com

"

The sparse, sublime instrumentation never takes the focus away from Cohen's inimitable voice, which is lush, deadpan, warm and poetic, with a hint of frailty adding to the sense of a final statement.

"

Dave Simpson,
The Guardian, on the final recordings

Leonard Cohen: *Thanks for the Dance* review
by Dave Simpson, *The Guardian*, November 22, 2019,
theguardian.com

CHAPTER
SIX

WIT AND WISDOM

A collection of Leonard Cohen's own words – and those of others – describing the great writer, his thoughts, experience and work.

That was my therapy, when I was depressed and sick. I'd read things… or listen to Leonard Cohen, which would actually make it worse.

Kurt Cobain
on what he did when feeling bad

interview with Jennie Punter, Impact, 1993, reproduced in nirvanaclub.com

> **"**
> I'm sorry I couldn't have spoken to the young man… There are always alternatives, and I might have been able to lay something on him.
> **"**

Leonard Cohen
on Kurt Cobain

Leonard Cohen on Kurt Cobain's Nirvana lyric name-check by Christopher Hooton, *The Independent*, November 11, 2016, independent.co.uk

"

He's so gentle and lovely and funny and gracious.

"

Producer **John Lissauer**
on Leonard Cohen

"Leonard Cohen's *New Skin for the Old Ceremony* at 45"
by Morgan Enos, Tidal, August 11, 2019,
tidal.com

I got into drugs and drinking and women and travel and feeling that I was part of a motorcycle gang or something.

Leonard Cohen
on the early years of touring

Leonard Cohen interview by *Uncut*,
February 26, 2015, uncut.co.uk

Most Played Songs on Tour

Bird on the Wire (635)
Suzanne (580)
Dance Me to the End of Love (539)
Who by Fire (516)
So Long, Marianne (515)
Hallelujah (504)
First We Take Manhattan (500)
I Tried to Leave You (478)
Everybody Knows (476)
I'm Your Man (474)

setlist.fm

Top 10 Songs

Hallelujah
Suzanne
Famous Blue Raincoat
Everybody Knows
Bird on a Wire
So Long, Marianne
Dance Me to the End of Love
Tower of Song
Anthem
I'm Your Man

"Readers' Poll: The 10 Best Leonard Cohen Songs"
by Andy Greene, November 26, 2014, rollingstone.com

The head of his record company said [of his album *Various Positions*], 'We can't release this.' And they didn't. Then, of course, [Hallelujah] got covered by the whole of humanity, much to Leonard's horror for a while. 99

Sylvie Simmons
on "Hallelujah"

"Remembering Leonard Cohen: biographer Sylvie Simmons on Montreal's beloved poet", interview with Eleanor Wachtel, CBC Radio, November 12, 2017, cbc.ca

"

This is an artist who worked on a single song – what would become 'Hallelujah' – for several years, writing 80 drafts and as many verses, only to have it rejected by his record label.

"

Adam Cohen
on his father's perseverance

interview, Scott Timberg with Adam Cohen, 2018,
theguardian.com

I think it is one of the best songs
I have written, maybe the best.
I knew that song was everything
that my whole work and life had
somehow gathered around. It is
absolutely true to me.

Leonard Cohen
on the song "Anthem"

"A touchstone for troubled times, Leonard Cohen's
'Anthem' took its own sweet time to happen" by
Brad Wheeler, *The Globe and Mail*, June 30, 2020,
theglobeandmail.com

66

I never discuss my mistresses or my tailors.

99

Leonard Cohen
on discretion, 2001

"I never discuss my mistresses or my tailors", interview
with Nick Paton Walsh, *The Observer*, October 14, 2001,
theguardian.com

To me, [the award] is like pinning a medal on Mount Everest for being the highest mountain. 🙶

Leonard Cohen
on Bob Dylan's Nobel Prize award

"Leonard Cohen responds to Bob Dylan Nobel Prize win"
by Samantha Maine, *NME*, October 15, 2016,
nme.com

66

We were like brothers, we lived on the same street and they all left empty spaces where they used to stand. It's lonesome without them.

99

Bob Dylan
on Leonard Cohen

"When Leonard Cohen described the 'strange event' of seeing Bob Dylan live", Far Out magazine, July 18, 2021, faroutmagazine.co.uk

I knew that something was
unfolding, and there was a
joyous activity behind it – but,
as I say, slightly crazed, which
freed the writing tremendously.
I was smoking grass and taking
acid from time to time.

Leonard Cohen
on the 1960s

interview with Mikal Gilmore, *Rolling Stone*, 2016,
rollingstone.com

"

I used to be petrified with the idea of going on the road and presenting my work. I often felt that the risks of humiliation were too wide.

"

Leonard Cohen
on performing his work, 1975

"Leonard Cohen: Cohen's New Skin" by Harvey Kubernik,
Melody Maker, March 1, 1975, rocksbackpages.com

All I've got to put in a song is my own experience. 99

Leonard Cohen
on songwriting

interview in *The Guardian*, January 2012,
concerttour.net